W9-AGW-356

How to Eat a Low-Salt Diet

Tips and Tricks to Help You with Low-Sodium Shopping, Cooking, and Restaurants

Jennifer Brannon, MD

ISBN-13: 978-0-9997991-1-6
ISBN-10: 0999799118

Disclaimer

While this book is written by a physician and has been well researched, it is not meant to be a substitute for medical advice from your medical professional. It contains hints and tips from my personal experience in learning to eat a low-sodium diet.

Talk with your doctor before you begin any exercise or diet program. Ask your doctor what your personal target sodium intake should be. Your doctor is familiar with your personal medical conditions and can give you the most informed recommendations.

In this book you will find references to Trademarks and brands. Each of these is property of each respective owner, and I have no affiliation with any of them. Brands mentioned are those that I have personally found at stores or tried, and I mention them to help the reader. Other options may be available and the listings are not meant to be exhaustive. New options are being produced all the time, and more options will likely become available after the publication of this book.

TABLE OF CONTENTS

ACKNOWLEDGMENTS

Many thanks to Kathryn Gray and Carolyn Brannon for proofreading my manuscript and offering suggestions. Thanks to John Brannon for help with technical support.

INTRODUCTION

You have probably heard by now that we all eat too much salt, and you may have tried to cut down on the amount of salt you eat. Many people think that they eat a low-salt diet but wonder why their health is not improving. This book will help you find the hidden sources of salt in your diet and provide you with tips and tricks to finally be able to stick to a low-salt diet once and for all!

Why am I passionate about teaching people this? I thought I was eating pretty well. After all, I am a physician and I knew what to do (or so I thought). But then I was diagnosed with Menière's disease in 2015. Hearing loss, tinnitus, and spinning vertigo rocked my world out of nowhere. I was told to eat less than 1,500mg/day of sodium. Ok, I thought…I don't add salt to my food…this should be easy.

But then I started paying attention to food labels and reading nutrition information when I went out to eat. Wow! I was so clueless about how to truly eat a low-sodium diet!

So, after a couple of years educating myself, I need to share this information. Everyone can eat this way, but there are some basic things that will help you learn the ropes.

Are you feeling overwhelmed? Are you not sure where to start? This book will give you the basic information you need to understand where the salt in our diet comes from. You will also find practical information to help you as you go grocery shopping and out to eat at restaurants. Although it takes a little bit of effort to change the way you eat, you CAN do it! You'll be surprised how much you will learn and how easy some of the changes can be.

CHAPTER 1

Why try to lower the salt in your diet?

There are many reasons why you might choose to start a low-salt diet. Many people have had a doctor recommend that they "cut back on salt" to help with blood pressure or heart issues. Some have chronic kidney problems and are supposed to limit salt for that reason. Some have inner ear problems like Menière's, a disease that is supposed to be better controlled by eating less salt.

Yet other people choose to limit salt to lead a healthier lifestyle. They realize that we all eat too much salt in our daily diets and they want to change.

Whatever your reasons for wanting to limit salt in

your diet, you are reading a book that will ease your transition to lower salt and make it much easier for you to stick with it. You may be making many changes in your diet...or you may just be choosing to change one thing at a time. Now is the time to eat less salt, and this book will help guide you!

In the pages ahead, you will find easy-to-read information about sodium in our diets. You will find bullet points for different categories of foods and great ideas about how you can reduce the amount of sodium in your diet. You will also find ideas for what to eat when you go out to eat at restaurants. Don't be overwhelmed by needing to read a huge textbook to figure it out! Use this book instead!

CHAPTER 2

The Basics – Let's talk about Salt

First things first. We need to discuss some of the basics of salt. What is it? How much should we eat? Can we just skip it altogether?

Salt is added to food to add flavor and serve as a preservative. It has been used for thousands of years for both reasons.

Sodium Chloride is one of the most common types of salt in our foods. It is also known as table salt. Here are the approximate amounts of sodium in table salt:

- ¼ teaspoon salt = 575 milligrams of sodium
- ½ teaspoon salt = 1,150 milligrams of sodium

- ¾ teaspoon salt = 1,725 milligrams of sodium
- 1 teaspoon salt = 2,300 milligrams of sodium

But, there are many other kinds of sodium in our foods as well. Different kinds of sodium are found in many different foods. Things like sodium bicarbonate (baking soda), sodium citrate, sodium nitrate, sodium benzoate, and monosodium glutamate (MSG) all contain sodium. In order to reap the health benefits from a low "salt" diet, we must look for all of these. We need to focus on a low-sodium diet, not just a low-salt diet.

Our bodies need a small amount of sodium to function properly. Sodium helps balance the fluids in our cells and helps our muscles contract well. The current recommendations from the Centers for Disease Control state that people should consume less than 2,300 milligrams (mg) of sodium per day, but most people are eating much more than this. Some restaurant meals include this many milligrams of sodium in one meal. Many people are consuming more than 3,000mg/day and some even have more than 6,000-7,000mg/day in their diet.

The American Heart Association goes a step further and recommends that people eat less than 1,500mg/day.

You can talk with your doctor about how much salt you should consume, but a good rule of thumb to start with is to aim for less than 2,300mg/day. Conditions like heart failure, kidney disease, and Menière's disease may require a stricter diet of 1,000-1,500mg/day.

Some people are able to "save up" their sodium amount for the day and eat it mostly in one meal. Others, like patients with Menière's disease or kidney problems need to keep their sodium levels more stable. They should aim to eat around 500mg sodium per meal.

CHAPTER 3

Reading Labels

You might think that by not picking up the salt shaker you have truly started your low-sodium journey. While this is a step in the right direction, the salt shaker is not where most of the sodium in your diet is coming from.

To truly understand and identify the sodium in your diet, you need to learn to read package labels. It is important that you understand where to find the information about sodium and how to interpret it.

One place you can look is the ingredient list. Here is a list of food ingredients that contain sodium.

- Salt
- Sea salt
- Kosher salt
- Himalayan pink salt
- Rock salt
- Sodium bicarbonate
- Sodium nitrate
- Sodium chloride
- Sodium citrate
- Sodium glutamate
- Sodium phosphate
- Sodium lactate
- Sodium diacetate
- Sodium erythorbate
- Sodium lauryl sulfate
- Sodium metabisulfite
- Trisodium phosphate
- Monosodium glutamate (MSG)
- Disodium guanylate (GMP)
- Disodium inosinate (IMP)
- Fleur de sel

Most package labels include information about sodium, usually listed on the label with the other ingredients like protein, carbohydrates, and fats. This tells you how many milligrams of sodium you can find in a serving. This is important!

Here is an example:

Nutrition Facts	
Serving Size 10 crackers (20g)	
Servings per container about 8	

Amount Per Serving	
Calories 120	Calories from Fat 60

	% Daily Value
Total Fat 6g	14%
Saturated Fat 1g	6%
Trans Fat 0g	
Cholesterol 0g	0%
Sodium 155mg	6%
Total Carbohydrate 20g	7%
Dietary Fiber less than 1g	4%
Sugars 0g	
Protein 2g	

Vitamin A 0%	*	Vitamin C 0%
Calcium 0%	*	Iron 0%

*Percent Daily Values are based on a 2,000-calorie diet. Your daily values may be higher or lower depending on your calorie needs:

	Calories:	2,000	2,500
Total Fat	Less Than	65g	80g
Sat Fat	Less Than	20g	25g
Cholesterol	Less Than	300mg	300mg
Sodium	Less Than	2,400mg	2,400mg
Total Carbohydrate		300g	375g
Dietary Fiber		25g	30g

Let's talk about this label. It may seem intimidating, but here are the things to look at and focus on. Serving size and sodium are most important when considering your sodium intake.

- **<u>Serving size</u>** - You need to look at the top of the label and see what the serving size is! This tells you how much you can eat for a specific amount of the food, calories, or milligrams of sodium. One piece of bread is a serving, and it can have anywhere between 80 to over 200 milligrams of sodium…in one slice! If you eat a sandwich with two slices of bread, you need to make sure you are multiplying the sodium amount by two.

Here is where you find the serving size on our example label:

Nutrition Facts
Serving Size 10 crackers (20g)
Servings per container about 8

Many breakfast cereals have at least 150 milligrams (mg) per serving, which is usually 1/2 - 3/4 cup of cereal. If you fill a huge bowl with cereal, you are having several servings and so the amount of sodium you end up eating is much higher.

- **<u>Sodium</u>** – The number of milligrams (mg) of sodium listed should be added to your daily amount. Just remember to make sure you are adding the correct amount for the serving size that you eat. You can eat more than one serving of some foods, just don't forget to double or triple the milligrams of sodium that you keep track of if you eat more than one serving. On our example label, it looks like this:

Sodium 155mg	6%

- **Calories** – If you are trying to watch your weight, this is important. Higher calorie foods should be limited in quantity. The good news is that the calories per serving do not really influence your sodium intake.

Amount Per Serving	
Calories 120	Calories from Fat 60

- **Protein** – Proteins do not affect sodium intake, but most protein-containing foods do contain some sodium. Things like eggs, meat, nuts, and dairy all contain some protein. Protein helps you have energy and helps you feel full longer. It also helps blood sugar stay more stabilized.

Protein 2g

- **Fats** – The amount of fats does not affect the sodium in the food, but if you're trying to eat a healthier diet it is something to pay attention to. Aim for less fat and avoid saturated and trans fats.

	% Daily Value
Total Fat 6g	14%
Saturated Fat 1g	6%
Trans Fat 0g	

- **Carbohydrates** – Carbohydrates give you energy and are converted to sugars in your body. These do not affect the sodium in your diet, but if you are trying to lose weight and become healthier you will want to avoid overeating carbs. A general rule is: fiber is good, but simple sugars are bad.

Total Carbohydrate 20g	7%
Dietary Fiber less than 1g	4%
Sugars 0g	

- **Cholesterol** – The amount of cholesterol on the label will not tell you about your sodium intake. This number can be important when considering a healthy diet, but more information on this can be found in other sources.

Cholesterol 0g	0%

- **Table at the bottom** - What is that weird looking table at the bottom of the label? It is just that: a table that tells people how much to eat of each item based on a certain calorie diet. For example, they usually include a 2,000 and a 2,500 diet and they tell you how much fat, carbs, and sodium is recommended based on your calorie intake. Usually the percentages (%) listed on the label are based on a 2000 calorie diet. If you are eating fewer calories per day, your percentage will be different than what they list.

*Percent Daily Values are based on a 2,000-calorie diet. Your daily values may be higher or lower depending on your calorie needs:

	Calories:	2,000	2,500
Total Fat	Less Than	65g	80g
Sat Fat	Less Than	20g	25g
Cholesterol	Less Than	300mg	300mg
Sodium	Less Than	2,400mg	2,400mg
Total Carbohydrate		300g	375g
Dietary Fiber		25g	30g

I'll give a quick example. On our example label, a serving size is 10 crackers for 155 mg of sodium. They say this is 6% of the daily sodium intake a person should have based on 2,400mg of sodium per day. If your diet needs to be more strict, you would have to ignore the percentage that they give. (For a 1,500mg/day sodium intake, this serving of crackers is 10% of your total day intake of sodium.) If you want to eat 20 crackers instead of 10, you would be consuming 310 mg of sodium (155mg x 2 servings).

(Don't forget: As well as looking at the amount of sodium in a serving and paying attention to the serving size, remember, it is always a good idea to look at the ingredient list on the package.)

CHAPTER 4

Hidden Salt

Salt from a salt shaker is not the primary source of sodium in most peoples' diets. Many people think that by not adding salt at the dinner table, they are eating a low-salt diet. What they don't realize is that there are many sources of "hidden" salt. Some are truly hidden, as the user would not have any idea that there was sodium in the item unless they took the time to read the label. Some are just natural foods that we do not realize have sodium in them.

Natural Sources

Natural foods are some of the healthiest options for people watching their sodium intake, but there are some natural foods that have sodium in them. They are not a huge source of sodium, and these foods are usually healthy for you. I am including them in the interest of completeness and for those that are on a very strict sodium diet. Even though they do not have large amounts of sodium, the amounts will need to be added when keeping a running tally of the daily sodium you consume.

Dairy products are one surprising source of sodium that many people do not realize. **Milk** contains sodium in varying amounts depending on the brand and type. Make sure you read the label and serving size. You can count on 8 ounces of milk having at least 120 milligrams of sodium.

Yogurt is another source of sodium that many people have not thought of. One serving size usually has at least 80 milligrams, but many have even higher amounts. **Sour cream** and **ice cream** also include sodium in their ingredient lists in varying amounts.

Butter can be found with or without salt. One must buy unsalted butter (not margarine!) in order to avoid adding significant amounts of sodium when cooking and baking.

An **egg** has around 70 milligrams of sodium, but most of that is found in the white. Eat just the yolk and you can drastically reduce that number.

There are some fresh vegetables that have sodium naturally. These include **celery, beets, spinach, tomatoes, and carrots**. It is worth noting that the amount of sodium in these foods is not great, and they are very healthy foods to consume.

Baking Ingredients

Many processed foods have too much sodium. So, what is the solution? Should you make all your baked goods at home? Did you ever think about your baking ingredients having sodium in them? Does that birthday cake or muffin have too much sodium?

Two of the worst offenders are **baking powder** and **baking soda**. Baking soda contains 320 milligrams of sodium for every ¼ teaspoon that is added to the mixture. Baking powder contains 122 milligrams for every ¼ teaspoon. You can see how a recipe that requires a teaspoon or two of one or each of these could add up in a hurry. Couple this with salted butter, milk and some salted nuts and you could be in trouble!

Medications

There are some medications that contain sodium. Make sure to ask your pharmacist about the sodium content if you take medicines like: **erythromycin, ranitidine, didanosine, ticarcillin, piperacillin, carbenicillin, or cefamandol**. There are also some over the counter (OTC) medicines that contain sodium. Look at the ingredient list and look for words like "soda" or "sodium". If you are wondering about your medicines, don't hesitate to ask your pharmacist. They can give you exact amounts of sodium in your dose. (Declaring the Sodium Content of Drug Products, A Szarfman, N Engl J Med, 1995;333:1291)

Processed Foods

We have already mentioned several times that processed foods contain large amounts of sodium. What is a processed food, you ask? Anything that has been prepared and packaged. Many of them come in bottles, boxes, bags, and containers. Things that have a long shelf-life and have been prepared so they last a long time are usually processed. They are typically found down most central aisles of a grocery store.

Cereal, crackers, bread, sauces, and pre-

packaged meals are all processed foods. Processed meats have some of the highest levels of sodium. If you are used to eating **lunchmeat, sausage, bacon, ham, and turkey**, your diet is full of sodium. Read the labels to see how much you are getting. **Canned and packaged soups** also have large amounts of sodium.

It is hard to get away from processed foods due to the way most of us eat. In the next chapter, you will find some tricks and ideas about how to eat while making smart choices and some lower-sodium alternatives to the typical processed foods we have become accustomed to. Keep reading and you will find practical ideas!

Sauces and Condiments

So, you avoid heavily processed foods and the salt shaker and you should be good to go, right? Wrong! Even if you make great food choices and prepare things from scratch, you may be sabotaging your efforts by adding sauces and condiments.

Salad dressings are a fun way to make eating a salad delicious, and salads are a great low-sodium food! But, adding too much salad dressing may make your salad chock full of the sodium you were trying to avoid. Just 2 tablespoons of some salad dressings can pack a 300mg punch of sodium. Aim for low-sodium options and vinaigrettes. Better yet, use vinegar and oil.

Mayonnaise, ketchup, mustard, and pickles all make a hamburger taste great, but they are all full of sodium. Aim to reduce the amounts you put on your food, and eliminate all that are not necessary. Just pick one or two favorites. Try substituting other lower sodium options, and prepare your burgers with minced garlic and other spices for more flavor.

Soy sauce makes that Chinese food really yummy, but read the label and you'll find out that even a low-sodium option has 530 milligrams in one tablespoon. Other sauces like **Worcestershire sauce** also pack some sodium into the meal.

Soda Pop

Now, I know that this section is going to step on some toes, but in the interest of full disclosure we need to talk about carbonated beverages. Some people "cannot live" without their daily ice-cold **soda or cola beverages**. I am not going to go into the possible other health side effects of drinking these on a regular basis because I believe that there is already enough information in the media for any interested person to find this out for themselves.

But, we are going to jump into talking about the sodium content of the sodas. Some believe that by drinking diet soda, they are being more healthful. And if you are talking about amounts of sugar included, you would be correct (although you also should consider the artificial sweeteners). But did you know that if you drink diet soda you have really increased the amount of sodium that you are consuming?

Just one 8-ounce serving of some popular diet sodas can have as much as 100 mg of sodium. This is not a huge amount, but if you are trying to limit your sodium intake this is a number you need to consider (especially if you have several cans of soda each day).

CHAPTER 5

Practical Tips for Shopping

Now, you may be getting discouraged, but don't despair. You do not have to stop eating all of these foods! The idea is that you start to realize where the sodium you are eating is coming from....and you can choose what to keep eating. If you love ketchup on your burger, put some on it. Just skip the pickle and salty chips. Or if you love Chinese food, prepare your own at home or order it without sauce. You can use the lowest-sodium version you can find and use the sauce sparingly. This book is about giving you options to continue to enjoy eating while making it possible for you to meet your sodium intake goals! So, let's get into some specific tips while grocery shopping!

Grocery Shopping

Shop the Edges

As we have already discussed, processed foods are some of the worst things to choose when trying to avoid sodium in our diets. So, what do you do when the grocery store is full of them? You shop the edges of the grocery store.

By doing most of your shopping around the outer edges of the store you will be able to find the fresh fruits and vegetables, bread, and dairy products that will help your diet be successful. Obviously, you will still need to purchase things from those middle aisles with the boxes and containers, but if you aim to do the bulk of your purchases from fresh or frozen low-salt items you will be well on your way to achieving your goals of a low-sodium diet.

No/Low-Salt Alternatives

Do you feel like you are missing out on some of your favorite foods? Do you wish you could still eat some of the things you love? Well, many foods have a low-salt or no-salt alternative available! Here are some lists of no-salt and low-salt foods with brands and stores mentioned, as much as possible. The list is not comprehensive; it has been compiled based on my research and experience. Because stores change their merchandise, I cannot guarantee that your store will stock these. (Hint: Don't want to go shopping or can't find these in your local store? Many of these items are available to order online as well!)

No-Salt Foods List (And Where to Find Them)

- **Baking Powder** – Find Hain® no-sodium baking powder at Whole Foods Market®. Be careful with this if you take diuretics or have kidney issues, as they replace the sodium with potassium!
- **BBQ Sauce** – Mr. Spice® Honey BBQ Sauce is available online from HealthyHeartMarket.com
- **Bouillon** – Herb Ox® Chicken or Beef Bouillon Sodium-free is available at HealthyHeartMarket.com
- **Bread** – Look in your local grocery store's freezer for Ezekiel 4:9® sprouted-grain bread if you truly want a no sodium version.
- **Canned beans** – Find "no salt added" black, pinto, and kidney beans at local stores. You may even find generic versions available (Dillon's Food Stores®, Walmart®).
- **Canned fruits** – Items like applesauce, peaches, mandarin oranges, and pears are usually sodium-free or only contain very small amounts of sodium.
- **Canned tomatoes** – You can find canned tomatoes without added salt at local stores

like Dillon's Food Stores® and Walmart®, and they usually even stock these in the generic store brands. Just look for it to say, "no salt added". These will have a small amount of natural sodium even if they have not added any salt to the contents.

- **Canned vegetables** – You can find canned green beans, corn, and peas without salt at local stores like Dillon's Food Stores® and Walmart®, and they usually even stock these in the generic store brands. Just look for it to say, "no salt added" and make sure to read the label to make sure there truly is no salt.

- **Chili seasoning** – Williams® brand and Mrs. Dash® both have a no-salt version of their chili seasoning. Dillon's Food Stores® and Walmart® both carry the Williams® brand.

- **Crunchy Taco Shells** – You can find sodium-free crunchy shells at Aldi®. (Just be careful to watch your labels if you shop at other stores because most other brands do include sodium in their taco shells.)

- **Curry Sauce** – Mr. Spice® Indian Curry Sauce is available from HealthyHeartMarket.com

- **Fresh fruits and vegetables!!! Buy them anywhere!**

- **Frozen vegetables** – Most grocery stores have multiple varieties of frozen vegetables like corn, green beans, broccoli, cauliflower, etc. Just check the label to make sure it is salt-free. Avoid any vegetables with added sauces or cheese.

- **Honey Mustard** – Mr. Spice® Honey Mustard Sauce is available online at HealthyHeartMarket.com
- **Hot Sauce** – Mr. Spice® Tangy Bang Hot Sauce is available online at HealthyHeartMarket.com
- **Ketchup** – Both Heinz® and Hunts® offer a No-salt-added version. Use caution with Heinz® if you need to watch your potassium intake (Target®). Hunts® does not contain potassium (Amazon® or Walmart®).
- **Meatloaf Seasoning** – Mrs. Dash® has a sodium-free seasoning mix for meatloaf.
- **Mustard** – East Shore® Sweet and Tangy Mustard is available online at HealthyHeartMarket.com
- **Pickles** – You can find some no-salt dill pickles online at HeartHealthyMarket.com
- **Potato Chips** – Believe it or not, there are chips with no salt! Look for Guy's®, Kettle®, Art and Mary's® brands. Search at Dillon's Food Stores® or ask at your local grocery store. They might be willing to stock them for you.
- **Peanut butter** – There are several brands of "no salt added" peanut butter. They tend to

be more "natural" or "organic" kinds. You can search online to find one available near you or order one online. Some stores allow you to make your own peanut butter in the store.

- **Popsicles** – Buy popsicles made from fruit. Most grocery stores carry these.
- **Pot Roast Seasoning** – Mrs. Dash® has a pot roast seasoning mix that does not contain sodium.
- **Relish** – Alberto's® Sweet Jalapeño Relish is available online at HealthyHeartMarket.com
- **Seasonings** – Mrs. Dash®, Weber®, McCormick®, Lawry's®, AlsoSalt®, LoSalt®, and NoSalt® brands all have seasonings. (See the section on Seasonings in this chapter for more information.)
- **Sloppy Joe Seasoning** – Look for the sodium-free Mrs. Dash® Sloppy Joe seasoning mix online.
- **Taco Seasoning** – Mrs. Dash® has a no-salt version of taco seasoning. I have found this at my local Dillon's Food Stores® (Kroger®) and Walmart®.
- **Tortilla Chips** – Look at your local store for no-salt tortilla chips. (I have found the 365 Everyday Value® brand at Whole Foods Market® or Xochitl® brand at Walmart®).

- **Unsalted nuts** (cashews, peanuts, almonds, sunflower seeds, etc.) – available at many grocery stores. You may have to get them from the area where you weigh out an amount that you want from bins or barrels (Dillon's Food Stores®, Sprouts Farmers Market, Inc®). It seems a little more difficult to find them prepackaged in containers or jars, but it is possible. Aldi® has a great selection of pre-packaged nuts without salt at affordable prices.

Low-Salt Food List

- **Canned beans** – In addition to the "no salt added" cans we discussed in the previous section, you can find cans of beans that have "less sodium" or "reduced sodium". These are not the lowest sodium option, but they have less than a normal can of beans. Open the can and rinse the beans in water to lower the sodium content more. Most grocery stores carry these.
- **Canned vegetables** – We already discussed that you can find "no salt added" cans in the previous section, but if you are not restricting sodium as much, you can find "reduced sodium" cans that have a bit more sodium in them (while less than normal). Many have about 50% less than a normal

can of vegetables. Most grocery stores carry these.

- **Chicken Broth** – Look for a low-sodium (no salt added) version of chicken broth to help make those yummy soups for the winter. You might have to look at a specialty store or find an organic option to make sure it is truly low-sodium. Don't fall for the ones that say, "lower sodium" …. while these are better than the original versions, they are not truly "low-sodium".

- **Corn Tortillas** – These are typically low-sodium. You can find these at many grocery stores. Eating two of these can only have 10-20mg of sodium. Choose these instead of flour tortillas which can pack 110mg each!

- **Crackers** – Several brands of crackers (Wheat Thins®, Ritz Crackers®) have a lower sodium version. Take some time to browse the section and look for low-sodium options.

- **Granola bars** – The low-sodium granola bars that I have found are the organic ones at Aldi®. They only contain 10 milligrams of sodium each.

- **Lunchmeat** – So, when you try to limit sodium in your diet, lunchmeat is one thing that should automatically be cut out or limited. I have found some low-sodium deli turkey for when you are craving a deli sandwich. Look for Diestel Turkey Ranch® brand of turkey (Whole Foods Market®) and you can find several flavors of low-sodium turkey. You can also find varieties of Boar's Head® brand of lunchmeats (Sprouts Farmers Market, Inc®) which have lower sodium than the normal ones. (These are not as low as the Diestel no-sodium-added ones.) Some brands of organic, uncured meats have lower sodium than regular lunchmeat – you will just need to read the labels.

- **Olives -** Lindsay® Low-sodium Olives are available online at HealthyHeartMarket.com
- **Potato Chips** – There are multiple brands of potato chips that have reduced sodium. Look for packaging that says, "lower sodium", "low-salt" or "reduced-sodium".
- **Poultry** – Make sure to look for fresh or frozen poultry that has not been injected with a sodium solution. If it says "brine", "broth", or "salt solution", then it has been injected with added sodium. Either fresh or organic versions are most likely to be low-sodium.
- **Salad dressings** – You can find low-sodium vinaigrettes at local grocery stores like Dillon's Food Stores®, Aldi®, Sprouts Farmers Market, Inc®, and Walmart®.
- **Soup** – More stores are starting to carry low-sodium or no-salt added soups. Spend

some time in the natural/organic sections and look through the aisles. I've found chicken noodle, butternut squash, and tomato soups without added salt.

- **Tortilla Chips** – Look at your local store for a low-sodium or lightly-salted tortilla chip. (Whole Foods Market®)

Seasonings

Natural

- Use lemons, limes, and oranges to ramp up the flavor in your foods.
- Spices like cumin, garlic powder, pepper, curry, turmeric, cinnamon, nutmeg, ginger, and vinegar can all make foods more flavorful. Avoid garlic salt and onion salt.
- Onions and garlic can add great flavor to your food.
- Hot peppers or chili pepper flakes can add dimension and flavor to many dishes without adding salt.
- Make your own fresh salsa or Pico de Gallo for some flavor. Just leave out the salt.

Prepackaged

- AlsoSalt® is a salt substitute.

- Dr. Rhoden's Flavor Doctor® has several seasonings.
- Kirkland® has an organic no-salt seasoning.
- Lawry's® has a Salt-Free 17 Seasoning and a Salt-Free Mexican Seasoning.
- Lo-salt® is a salt substitute that has 66% less sodium than regular salt. NoSalt® is a sodium-free salt alternative. You can use this on food or in baking. Just be careful if you need to monitor your potassium levels (heart and kidney patients), as potassium is substituted for the missing sodium. Check with your doctor to make sure this is ok for you to use.
- McCormick® also has a Garlic and Herb Salt-Free Seasoning and an Original All-Purpose Salt-free seasoning that works well in cooking and grilling.
- Mickey & T's Gourmet has several seasonings.
- Morton® Salt Substitute is another option.
- Mrs. Dash® is the no-salt seasoning that many people have heard of, but you may not be aware that there are multiple varieties. I have seen these in Walmart®, Sam's Club®, and Dillon's Food Stores® and online.
- Weber® has several salt-free seasonings that are very tasty and can be used in cooking or marinades for grilling. Try the chicken,

steak, or burger varieties. Try looking for these at Walmart® or Sam's Club®.

CHAPTER 6

Cooking at Home – Tips and Tricks

As you begin your journey of eating less sodium, you will probably begin cooking and preparing more of your food at home. Here are some tips for how to cook at home without using lots of salt.

- Do not salt water for boiling pasta. You will likely have other seasonings or sauces on it when you eat it and you will not miss the added salt.
- Do not salt rice while cooking.
- Avoid canned "cream of ..." soups (like mushroom or chicken). You can look online for a recipe to make your own if you're feeling adventurous.
- Use corn tortillas when making enchiladas, tacos or burritos.

- Do not cook with ham, bacon, sausage or other cured meats.
- Buy salt-free seasonings (or make your own) for things like tacos, chili, and marinades.
- Add natural fruits and vegetables to enhance flavor. Use lemons, limes, oranges, onions, garlic, etc. in your cooking.
- Roasting vegetables is a great way to add flavor.
- Rinse canned beans and vegetables to reduce sodium.
- Avoid garlic salt and onion salt.
- Use salt substitutes if your doctor has approved them.
- Use no-salt seasonings or spice mixtures to marinade meats.
- You can substitute ground flax seed in a recipe that calls for an egg when making bread or muffins.
- Use salt-free baking powder when baking.
- Leave salt out of recipes for cookies, muffins, and breads. You probably won't notice the difference.
- Look for recipes with fruit to make your desserts. A good apple, peach or blueberry crisp is delicious and can be made salt-free (just make sure you use unsalted butter).
- Try using a bread machine to make breads and doughs without added salt. You might discover that making homemade pizza

dough or cinnamon rolls by using this handy appliance is easier than you thought! (And you can control the ingredients and leave the salt out!)

CHAPTER 7

Eating Out - General Rules

Eating out on a low-sodium diet can be discouraging and downright frustrating, but I hope to give you some ideas to make it a little more enjoyable.

1. **Look for a menu online before you go.** There is nothing worse than sitting there staring at a menu and thinking, "I have no idea what I can order that does not have too much salt". If you look at a menu ahead of time, you can see if there is nutrition information available and already know what your options are. This is also helpful if there are limited options. You may need to pack some food (fresh fruit, veggies, salad dressing) to take with you to the restaurant

to supplement your meal. This can be frustrating and embarrassing, but it is better than not eating or consuming too much sodium and getting sick later.

2. **Don't be afraid to ask for nutritional information at the restaurant.** Worst case scenario is that they don't have the info. Some restaurants may not have information online, but they will allow you to look at it inside the restaurant. Some will only verbally tell you the nutritional content of certain dishes that you ask about. Be brave! This may take a couple of extra minutes before you order, but finding something that you can eat without worrying about becoming ill afterwards is worth it.

3. **See if you can have your food prepared to order.** You may need to ask the server if the meat can be cooked to order and without salt. Many restaurants already have their meat marinated or precooked so this is not possible. Whenever you can, ask to have it prepared without salt. (Of course, there is no guarantee that the cook will actually comply with this request, but it is worth asking. If you are truly on a low-sodium diet for a specific health reason, it may be best to skip this altogether if you can't be sure.) Hint: If your salad comes with cold, sliced chicken on it, it has been marinated

and prepared ahead of time and is probably not low in sodium.

4. **Eat salad or fresh veggies.** This sounds very unromantic, I know. But, this is one way you can ensure you are not getting filled up with sodium. (You'll have to leave off the bacon, cheese, pickled onions, croutons, tortilla strips, etc.) Having a bowl of fresh lettuce, tomatoes, cucumber, carrots, avocado, and even an egg will help you stay under your sodium goal.

5. **Bring your own salad dressing.** Don't sabotage your salad! If you are going to try to eat healthily and low-sodium, don't let the restaurant drench it in high sodium dressing. Just 2 Tablespoons of some salad dressings can have more than 300mg of sodium. If you forget your own, ask for vinegar and oil or go for the vinaigrette option. Make sure you get it on the side and use it sparingly. Stay away from ranch or cheese-based dressings. (Hint: Dipping the tip of your fork in the dressing before putting salad on your fork for the next bite is a simple way to limit the amount of dressing you take in while getting some of the flavor.)

6. **Look for a baked potato.** Only add butter and/or sour cream, and make sure the outer peeling is not covered in salt. Say no to the cheese and bacon to cut your sodium intake.

7. **Never eat bacon or lunchmeat when out.** Enough said.

8. **Do not eat pickles or pickled items.**

9. **Don't eat French fries or chips.** You might be able to find a Mexican restaurant that has corn tortilla chips without salt, but you'll have to ask. They may be able to make you a special batch. You might be able to ask about making a batch of French fries without salt, too.

10. **Choose corn tortillas instead of flour.** Just one corn tortilla has around 10 mg of sodium, but its flour counterpart can have 10 times that much (over 100mg of sodium).

11. **Leave off the bread.** I know…this is a hard one for us bread-lovers. But if you order a hamburger cooked to order without salt, the meat already has some natural salt in it. Depending on what you put on the burger, you are adding more sodium. Did you know that the bun can add another 100-500mg of sodium? And those yummy breadsticks, garlic breads, and croissants that come with your meal? Those alone very likely contain the amount of sodium that you should have for the entire meal.

12. **Don't be afraid to pick and choose your condiments.** It's ok to ask for your veggie sub sandwich without mayo and mustard or to ask for your hamburger to be plain or only have lettuce and tomato on it.

13. **Use lemons and limes to add flavor.** Most restaurants have both available and you can squeeze these onto salads and meats to increase the flavor and enjoyment.

14. **Pack your own food when necessary.**

Going to a potluck? Going to someone's house for dinner? You can follow the same guidelines that we just discussed.

Better yet…offer to bring something to the meal, and cook something that is low-sodium that you KNOW you can eat! It may be the only thing you know for sure is safe.

CHAPTER 8

Eating Out - Where to Go?

So where can you get low-sodium food if you decide to eat out? In the following lists, I will try to tell you items that you can order for 500mg or less. (This allows for 500mg each at breakfast, lunch, and dinner.) The lists are not exact and are based on items available and information available at the time of publication. This list is not meant to be comprehensive, and there may be other options available as menu items change. Do a little research before you go!

Always check the online or listed nutritional content of the foods to be sure! (And don't forget to add in any sodium from soda pop or condiments that you might choose.) Usually online large restaurant chains will include their nutritional information online, so if you choose a local restaurant you'll probably have to ask them. If information is not available, follow the general guidelines in the previous chapter.

Some people can eat almost no sodium during the day and then eat their entire daily amount at dinner, but some need to keep an even amount of sodium in their bodies. If you have a little more leeway in your diet and you do not have to stick to a 1,500mg per day sodium intake you can have a little more freedom. Talk to your doctor about your optimum daily sodium intake.

Here are some practical options for the next time you want to eat out:

Fast food

- **Arby's®** - Eat half of an Arby's Melt and order applesauce as the side. Several desserts are fairly low sodium. See the information online.
- **Braum's®** – I have been told that some Braum's will cook your fries to order without salt if you request it. Many have a small grocery area attached to the restaurant and you can find fresh fruit and veggies to supplement your meal. Check the nutritional information for ice creams.

- **Burger King®** – Pick one: Whopper, Jr. ®, hamburger or double hamburger, or 6pc nuggets. Side salads are available. Applesauce is sodium-free and can help round out the meal. Try the oatmeal for breakfast. You can find more information online.

- **Carl's Jr.®** - Try the six-piece Chicken Stars™. Look online for more information.

- **Chester's®** - Try one chicken tender, leg, or wing. Look up the information online.

- **Chick-fil-a®** – Eat only 2 of 3 Chick-n-Minis™ or one Chicken Strip. Ask at the counter about low sodium options. They can tell you sodium content in their foods. Fruit cups are a great choice.

- **Church's Chicken®** - Try an original or spicy leg. You can choose 2 Tender Strips® instead. Their honey sauce does not add any extra sodium. Corn is a great low-sodium side. Look online for more information.

- **Culver's®** – Choose a side salad or Garden Fresco Salad with vinaigrette dressing. Many of their desserts are not terribly high in sodium. Check online for details.

- **Dairy Queen®** - Order a side salad with one chicken strip. Applesauce and bananas are also on the menu and can round out your meal without adding sodium. Many of the desserts have less than 500 mg sodium. Look online for nutritional information.

- **Fazoli's®** – You can eat a child portion of noodles with marinara sauce or a side salad. I recommend bringing your own dressing. Check more information online.

- **Freddy's Frozen Custard and Steakburgers®** – Try the California Style Steakburger without sauce or cheese. Skip the fries. Their custard is not very high in sodium. Check online if you want more information.

- **Green Burrito®** - Try a Crispy Beef Taco with a side of chips. Look online for information.

- **In-N-Out Burger®** – Choose a Protein® Style Burger (no bun) without condiments.

- **KFC®** - Choose one Original Recipe®, Extra Crispy™, or Kentucky Grilled Chicken® drumstick or chicken wing. Corn on the cob and the side salad are good low-sodium options. I recommend packing your own dressing.

- **Long John Silver's®** - Try the baked cod or shrimp, or the battered shrimp. Adding lemon juice doesn't add any sodium. If fish is not your thing, order the baked potato.

- **McDonalds®** – Pick one: oatmeal, small hamburger (without cheese), a Fruit 'n Yogurt parfait, or 4 Chicken McNuggets®. You can order an ice cream cone or sundae for under 500mg, too. Add some apple slices, if you'd like. Nutritional information is available online.

- **Orange Julius®** - Most of their smoothies are under 500mg sodium. Look online for information.

- **Panda Express®** – Their brown and white steamed rice are very low salt. According to their online information, you can have your choice of the Mixed Veggie (entrée), Sweet and Sour Chicken Breast, SweetFire Chicken Breast™, or Honey Walnut Shrimp. Several of the sides have less than 500mg if you'd rather not have an entrée. Remember that if you add any sauces, you'll be adding between 115-375mg sodium per serving.

- **Pollo Campero®** – Choose a drumstick or one of several kinds of empanadas. You could also choose a cup of Chipotle Rustica Soup. Add a couple of corn tortillas on the side.

- **Popeye's Louisiana Kitchen®** – Try the Handcrafted Nuggets® kid's meal with a corn on the cob cobbett or grits as the side. See the nutritional information online.

- **Raising Cane's Chicken Fingers®** – You can eat two chicken fingers or one chicken finger and fries. They also have their information online.

- **Slim Chickens®** – Try 2 fried or grilled chicken tenders (without sauce) or choose a side salad and one tender. Raspberry vinaigrette is the lowest sodium option. Applesauce is a no-sodium side. Information is online.

- **Smoothie King®** - All of their smoothies are under 500mg sodium. Look online for more information.
- **Sonic®** - Order a Jr. Burger without condiments and applesauce as the side. See the nutritional information online.
- **Taco Bell®** – Most of the tacos are under 500mg (you can order them Fresco style for less sodium) so eating one taco is an option. For breakfast, you could have one egg and cheese or sausage breakfast soft taco for 330-400mg. The menu of things for a dollar has several options under 500mg (spicy tostada, spicy potato soft taco, cheese roll-up) but, again, you could only have one. Don't forget that each hot sauce packet adds 30-150mg of sodium. Nutritional information is available online.
- **Taco Bueno®** – You can pick from: two party tacos, one Chicken Taco Rollup, a beef or crispy taco, or two steak crispy tacos. They also have applesauce on the menu. Information is online.
- **Taco Shop®** - Try one taco or beef or cheese enchilada. See information online.
- **Wendy's®** – Choose from a sour cream and chive baked potato, 4 chicken nuggets,

garden salad or a Frosty®. The half-size Power Mediterranean Chicken Salad comes close at 520mg. Apple slices are available as well. Nutritional information is available online.

- **Whataburger®** – Try either the Garden Salad or the Apple and Cranberry Salad. Apple slices are available as a sodium-free side. A cinnamon roll is a low-sodium breakfast option. You can find nutritional information online.

- **Zaxby's®** – Try a Garden House Zalad® or a Garden Cobb Zalad® (without the bacon and fried onions). Just don't eat the Texas Toast to stay under 500mg of sodium. I recommend packing your own dressing, or choose 1000 Island for the lowest sodium content. If you don't want a salad, you can eat one chicken strip or a side of chicken salad (no bun). They have very detailed nutritional information online.

Sandwiches

- **Jimmy John's®** – You can order a vegetarian sandwich without cheese and eat only half. ☺ Skip the chips or pack your own salt-free ones from home. Nutritional information is available online and you can "build" your own sandwich and see exactly what the nutritional content will be.

- **Potbelly Sandwich Shop®** – You can try their Chicken Salad Salad or a side of Classic Tomato soup. For breakfast they have great oatmeal options with several different toppings. Look online for more information.

- **Subway®** – The Veggie Delite® sandwich is only listed as having 280mg. Of course, if you add cheese, mayo, mustard, or ranch to it, the amount will increase pretty quickly (usually 100-200mg for each). For the lowest sodium, just add vinegar and oil or choose one condiment. They have a great online tool where you can calculate your nutritional info ahead of time. If you really want the taste of a lunchmeat sandwich, you'll have to order the "mini" version (for kids) to stay under 500mg.

Fast-Casual

- **Chipotle®** – You can stay under 500mg if you get a salad with chicken or steak and one other topping like brown rice or sour cream. Use limes instead of dressing or bring your own. If you want salsa, the green chile salsa has the least sodium. Ask for corn tortillas on the side. Check out the nutrition facts available in the store as you stand in line.

- **Five Guys®** – Now THIS is a restaurant where you can actually feel like you have gotten to eat a meal. Order the little hamburger with just lettuce and tomatoes and order the French fries without salt. They will cook them nice and fresh for you, and they will be hot and salt-free!

- **Fuddruckers®** – Try the Rib-eye Steak Sandwich or the 1/3-pound Original Burger with wheat small bun and top it only with lettuce and tomatoes.

- **The Habit Burger Grill®** – You could either order a Garden Salad or a Grilled Chicken Salad and pair it with your own dressing or pick one from their list online.

- **Jason's Deli®** – Pick half of one of these: Shelley's Deli Chick, Wild Salmon-wich, Zucchini Grillini, Spinach Veggie Wrap, or Gourmet Pimento Cheese Sandwich. Add a fruit cup to round out your meal. Another option is to make your own salad at the salad bar. Make sure you choose just fresh fruits and veggies and eggs; avoid the pasta salads, cottage cheese, bacon, croutons, cheese, little muffins, and crackers. Information is online.

- **Kneaders®** - Try the Large Green Avocado Half Salad at 505mg sodium. This is without dressing. Pack your own or choose poppyseed as the lowest. There are several kids sandwiches under 500mg sodium. For breakfast opt for the oatmeal or a chocolate croissant.

- **McAlister's Deli®** – Choose a Cheese Spud or you can have half of one of a few sandwiches or potatoes. There is applesauce and fruit available. Information is online.
- **Moe's Southwest Grill®** – Order two corn tortillas with chicken, lettuce, Pico de Gallo, and lime. You can build your own creations online and see the exact nutritional information for what you create.
- **Panera®** – For breakfast you can pick one: oatmeal, a muffin, or a bagel without cream cheese. Many of the half-salads are options, but make sure to check ahead of time (they have a book with the nutritional information available in restaurants). Get your salad dressing on the side and use only what you need. Skip the bacon, cheese, and pickled onions. Order apple instead of bread or chips as a side.
- **Qdoba®** – Order a corn tortilla with your choice of meat and top with lettuce, tomatoes, and lime juice. Add applesauce as a side.
- **Zoë's Kitchen®** – Choose a veggie kabob with fresh fruit as the side.

Casual Dining

- **Abuelo's®** – One great thing about Abuelo's is that their chips are very low-salt (about 20 mg per serving). Choose from one of their enchiladas (information online) and order only one a la carte or choose a cup of tortilla soup.

- **Applebee's®** – You can have a lunch-sized Caesar salad, a house salad without dressing, green beans, broccoli, or some of the desserts. Check out the information online for details about nutrition.

- **BJ's®** – Several mini deep-dish pizzas are less than 500mg each or you could eat a slice or two of a Tavern-cut pizza. Look online to choose one. If you'd rather, you could get the Classic Potato and choose one of the small salads. Applesauce and fresh fruit are available as sides.

- **Bonefish Grill®** – Try the filet mignon or one of the grilled fish entrées with greens on the side.

- **Captain D's Seafood Kitchen®** - Choose from the breaded flounder, Southern-style Fish Tenders, butterfly shrimp, or one of the grilled fish options. Broccoli and a baked potato is a great low-sodium option.

- **Carrabba's®** – Eat one-fourth of a wood-fired cheese pizza or a 6-ounce Tuscan Grilled Sirloin with steamed broccoli.

- **Cheddar's®** – Try the 6-ounce sirloin steak or choose a plate with several sides (sweet potato, broccoli, carrots). A house salad with your own dressing is another option. Look online for exact nutritional information.
- **The Cheesecake Factory®** – You could have a small green salad, a lunch portion of Rigatoni with Roasted Tomato Sauce, a lunch portion of Pasta da Vinci, or grilled fish (salmon, mahi, tuna) with broccoli and steamed white rice. Look online for more information.
- **Chili's®** – Try a cup of clam chowder. Low-sodium sides include mandarin oranges and pineapple. You can see the information online.
- **Colton's Steakhouse and Grill®** - Try a baked sweet potato with cinnamon and sugar with grilled asparagus on the side. You could choose sweet potato fries instead. There is applesauce on the kid's menu. Look online for more information.
- **Country Kitchen®** – Try a side salad with a side of red potatoes. Information is online.
- **Cracker Barrel®** – The apple cinnamon oatmeal, pork chop, or two eggs and grits each have less than 500mg of sodium. There are several sides you can add as well (applesauce, apples, broccoli). Avoid bacon, sausage, and biscuits or else your sodium content will be high. Several

desserts are fairly low in sodium. See full nutritional content online.

- **Denny's®** - Order two fried or boiled eggs with an English muffin. You can have grits on the side. Oatmeal and seasonal fruit is also a great choice. The 55+ Fit Fare® Loaded Veggie Omelette is also another option. The nutritional information is online.

- **Granite City Food and Brewery®** – Have a house salad with your own dressing or try a kid's portion of chicken or fish or a couple of sides (mashed potatoes and applesauce). Look online for more details.

- **Logan's Roadhouse®** – You can have a bowl of shrimp and corn chowder. Another option is a Caesar side salad or House salad with balsamic vinaigrette or house ranch dressing. If you'd rather have meat, you can have the 6-ounce sirloin steak. The lowest sodium sides are rice pilaf, cinnamon apples, and broccoli. Kid's grilled chicken or kid's popcorn shrimp are also under 500mg sodium.

- **Longhorn Steakhouse®** – Try the Strawberry and Pecan Salad with dressing. If you'd rather not eat salad, pick either the salmon or a 6 or 8-ounce Flo's Filet®. The 6-ounce sirloin steak is just slightly over the limit. In regards to sides, avoid the rice, bread and loaded items with sauces and try some fresh steamed asparagus or a plain baked potato. There is more information online.

- **Maggiano's Little Italy®** – Try a Caesar side salad. Information is online.
- **O'Charley's®** – Pick from the Cedar-Planked Salmon, House salad or a Cup of Chicken Tortilla Soup. Pair it with applesauce or mandarin oranges to round out the meal. Information is online.
- **Olive Garden®** – Try the spaghetti with meat sauce mini pasta bowl, salad without dressing, kid's rotini with marinara or one breadstick. Check online for full details.
- **On the Border®** – Try one spinach and mushroom enchilada with sour cream sauce, one ground beef enchilada with chile con carne sauce, one veggie crispy or soft taco, or a house salad without dressing. Their corn tortillas are only 15mg each so you could add one or two of these to your meal for a little more substance without too much extra sodium. Check online for full details.
- **Outback Steakhouse®** – Try a house salad and a sweet potato or you can check online information for other items. You could eat a small ribeye (request that they make it without salt).
- **P.F. Chang's®** – Try the Buddha's Feast Steamed or the Kid's Sweet and Sour Chicken. Check online for more information.

- **Red Lobster®** – Try the steamed lobster, wood-grilled tilapia, or one of the fresh fish entrées. Just avoid most of the sauces and toppings. The baked potato is a great side choice. Look online to pick your favorite.

- **Red Robin Gourmet Burgers and Brews®**– Try a cup of baked potato soup or a side salad with steamed broccoli and fruit salad as sides.

- **Texas Roadhouse®** – Try a cup of loaded baked potato soup, a side salad with your own dressing, or a Cesar side salad. You could also choose a sweet potato with butter and cinnamon with applesauce for the side. The 6-ounce sirloin steak is just over the 500mg limit. See more information online.

- **TGI Fridays®** – You can eat a house salad with your own dressing or a half-portion of the Bruschetta Chicken Pasta. The kid's portion of pasta and marinara with a side of fruit, mandarin oranges or side salad is another option.

- **Yard House®** – You can have a Mixed Field Greens Salad with your own dressing or for a heartier meal choose one of the grilled fish options paired with Jasmine Rice and Mango Papaya Salsa. Another option is one Asada Taco. There are also several options on the kid's menu. Look up more information online.

- **Zio's Italian Kitchen®** – Try a House Cesar Salad or House Salad with your own dressing. Instead you could choose the Grilled Tilapia with seasonal vegetables.

BBQ

- Most things at a BBQ restaurant have a lot of sodium. Try a baked potato with butter, sour cream, and chives. Just make sure they don't add any bacon or meat. Some restaurants have a small side salad available, too.

Pizza

- Pizzas are notoriously salty, but you can generally eat one piece of a cheese or veggie pizza. Check the nutritional information online. Make sure you don't add any pepperoni, sausage, ham, anchovies, olives, or bacon to the pizza because the sodium content will skyrocket.

Breakfast

- **Dunkin Donuts®** – Most of their donuts are in the 300-500mg range. They also have a couple of breakfast sandwiches under 500mg. Check online for more information.

- **IHOP®** – Try two eggs and some oatmeal or a 55+ Omelette with veggies.
- **Jimmy's Egg®** – You can make your own low-sodium omelette and include veggies like: potatoes, tomatoes, spinach, mushrooms, asparagus, onion, bell pepper, and avocado. You could choose, instead, to have a couple of eggs with fruit, oatmeal, or grits as the side. To see your other options, search their nutritional information online.
- **Krispy Kreme®** – You can find the nutritional information online for their donuts, but most are under 150mg.

All-You-Can-Eat/ Buffets

- **Golden Corral®** – They have an extensive online menu with several options for meat and sides without a lot of sodium. Check it out before deciding what to put on your plate. Fresh fruit is available. Avoid pre-prepared salads, sauces, gravies, and condiments.
- **Pizza Ranch®** – Most slices of pizza are less than 500 mg. Check online to see exact amounts. Sides of mandarin oranges, pineapple, grapes, applesauce hardly add any sodium.
- **Ryan's®**- There are quite a few entrées on the menu that have less than 500mg apiece. Check the serving sizes and actual

information online. Pair one with a baked or sweet potato and fresh fruit. Avoid lots of baked goods – choose one if you love them. Avoid pre-prepared salads, sauces, gravies, and condiments.

BONUS SECTION! RECIPES!

Cold Corn Dip

<u>Cook</u> 1 package frozen corn per instructions on package

<u>Cool</u> corn.

<u>Add</u>:

    ½ cup sour cream

    2 ounces finely shredded sharp cheddar cheese

    Handful of cilantro, chopped

    2 green onions, chopped

    1-2 jalapenos, finely chopped

Serve chilled with no-salt tortilla chips.

A ½ cup serving has approximately 120 mg sodium.

Taco Soup

<u>Add to slow cooker</u>:
2 cans "no-salt added" black beans
1 can "no-salt added" diced tomatoes
1 can "no-salt added" Rotel®
1 package sodium-free taco seasoning
1 package frozen corn

Cook on low 4-8 hours. (Recipe can be doubled.)
The entire slow cooker has only approximately 140mg of sodium.
Serve with chopped avocado, sprinkles of cheese, sour cream, and salt-free tortilla chips. Add red pepper chili flakes for more heat without the added salt.

Chicken Fried Rice

1 Egg
1 teaspoon oil
¾ cup water
4 teaspoons low-sodium soy sauce
1/8 teaspoon garlic powder
¼ cup chopped scallions, including tops
1 cup instant rice
1 cup chopped cooked chicken

Scramble the egg in the oil in a pan. Add water, soy sauce, garlic and scallions and bring it all to a boil.
Stir in the instant rice and cover. Remove from heat and let stand 5 minutes. Add chicken. Recipe may be doubled.
One fourth of the recipe contains approximately 220mg sodium. (Remember if you add more sauces, you add to your sodium amount.)

Chicken Soft Tacos

<u>Marinate</u> chicken breasts with your favorite no-salt marinade. I like to use a garlic and herb flavored one with the juice of ½ lime added. You could also use a sodium-free taco seasoning packet.

<u>Grill</u> chicken and slice into thin strips.

Add chicken to soft corn tortillas and top with lettuce, diced tomatoes, homemade guacamole and a squeeze of lime.

Each chicken taco has approximately 75 mg sodium.

(You can also add a little bit of shredded cheese and a spoon of sour cream for approximately 50-75mg more per taco. Adding store-bought salsa adds more sodium, too.)

Cheese Pizza

In an automatic bread machine, <u>combine</u> the following to make dough:

    1 cup water, room temperature

    1 teaspoon honey

    1 ½ teaspoons olive oil

    2 2/3 + 1/2 cups bread flour

    ½ teaspoon garlic powder

    ½ Tablespoon Italian seasoning (without salt)

    1 ¾ teaspoons yeast (active dry or bread machine)

Run <u>bread machine on dough cycle</u>.

When dough is done, remove from bread machine and spread out flat on large pan covered lightly in olive oil.

Spread 1 cup spaghetti <u>sauce</u> (no salt added) over dough.

Sprinkle 8 ounces of shredded <u>mozzarella</u> over pizza.

Bake at 425 degrees F for 12-16 minutes.

One eighth of the pizza has approximately 215mg sodium. (If you use regular spaghetti or pizza sauce instead of the no-salt-added variety, you'll increase your sodium to around 340mg per 1/8 of the pizza.)

Pumpkin Waffles

<u>Mix together and beat well</u> in large bowl:

    2 eggs

    ¼ packed brown sugar

    1 cup pumpkin puree

    1 2/3 cup milk

    4 Tablespoons of unsalted butter melted and cooled

<u>Add dry ingredients</u> that have been combined, gently folding them in:

    1 ½ cup flour

    3 teaspoons no-sodium baking powder *

    ½ teaspoon baking soda

    1 teaspoon cinnamon

    1 teaspoon nutmeg

    1 teaspoon ginger

Cook per waffle iron instructions. Makes approx. 6 large waffles.

Sodium per waffle is approximately 160 mg.

*Remember to be careful about using no-sodium baking powder if you need to watch your potassium intake.

Apple Crisp

6-8 apples, peeled, cored and sliced
1 cup brown sugar
1 cup oats
½ cup flour
1 teaspoon cinnamon
½ cup cold unsalted butter (1 stick), cut into small pieces

Grease a 9-inch baking dish. Add apples.
Mix brown sugar, oats, flour, and cinnamon in a separate bowl. Add the cold butter and mix into the dry ingredients until mixture is crumbly.
Add mixture on top of apples and bake at 350 F for 40 minutes.
This dessert is sodium-free unless you top it with other things like ice cream or whipped topping.

Oatmeal Raisin Muffins

<u>Cream together</u>:

> 1/3 cup shortening
>
> ½ cup brown sugar
>
> 1 egg

<u>Stir in</u>:

> 1 cup quick oats
>
> 1 cup sour milk (You can make this by adding 2 Tablespoons vinegar to regular milk)

<u>Sift together</u>:

> 1 cup sifted flour
>
> 1 teaspoon no-sodium baking powder *
>
> ½ teaspoon baking soda
>
> 1 teaspoon cinnamon
>
> ½ teaspoon cloves

<u>Optional</u>:

> 1 cup raisins
>
> ½ cup chopped apples

Beat well and add dry ingredients. Stir enough to moisten. Add 1 cup raisins and/or ½ cup chopped apples. Spray muffin pan or use paper liners. Fill each muffin 2/3 full of batter.

Bake at 400 degrees Fahrenheit for 20-25 minutes. Makes 12-16.

Sodium per muffin is approximately 70mg.

*Remember to be careful with no-sodium baking powder if you need to watch your potassium intake.

TABLES

In the following pages, you will find tables to help you monitor your sodium intake.

Pick the top <u>Changes</u> you want to make in your diet and write them down.

Practice filling out one <u>Daily Sodium Tracker</u> each day to start keeping track of your sodium.

Use the <u>Symptom Tracker</u> pages to jot down your daily sodium eaten and write down any symptoms you experience. Take this to show your doctor at your next visit.

My Changes

(Write down the first changes you want to implement in your diet.)

Change 1 _____

Change 2 _____

Change 3 _____

EXAMPLE Daily Sodium Tracker

(Fill in the table with each food item and its sodium content. Add up your daily total at the bottom.)

	Food Item	Sodium Content (mg)
Breakfast	1 cup milk	120mg
	2 eggs	(70mg each) 140mg
	1 piece of toast	120mg
	Unsalted butter	0
Snack	Apple	0
Lunch	2 pieces of bread	(120mg each) 240mg
	2 T. peanut butter	140mg
	Grapes	0
	Raisins	0
Snack	Low-salt Wheat Thins®	55mg
Dinner	Lettuce salad/tomato	15mg
	Salad Dressing	110mg
	Chicken Breast	105mg
	Brownie	220mg
Snack		
Medicines		0
Total:		1,265mg

Daily Sodium Tracker

(Fill in the table with each food item and its sodium
content. Add up your daily total at the bottom.)

	Food Item	Sodium Content (mg)
Breakfast		
Snack		
Lunch		
Snack		
Dinner		
Snack		
Medicines		
Total:		

Daily Sodium Tracker

(Fill in the table with each food item and its sodium
content. Add up your daily total at the bottom.)

	Food Item	Sodium Content (mg)
Breakfast		
Snack		
Lunch		
Snack		
Dinner		
Snack		
Medicines		
Total:		

Daily Sodium Tracker

(Fill in the table with each food item and its sodium
content. Add up your daily total at the bottom.)

	Food Item	Sodium Content (mg)
Breakfast		
Snack		
Lunch		
Snack		
Dinner		
Snack		
Medicines		
Total:		

Daily Sodium Tracker

(Fill in the table with each food item and its sodium
content. Add up your daily total at the bottom.)

	Food Item	Sodium Content (mg)
Breakfast		
Snack		
Lunch		
Snack		
Dinner		
Snack		
Medicines		
Total:		

Daily Sodium Tracker

(Fill in the table with each food item and its sodium content. Add up your daily total at the bottom.)

	Food Item	Sodium Content (mg)
Breakfast		
Snack		
Lunch		
Snack		
Dinner		
Snack		
Medicines		
Total:		

Daily Sodium Tracker

(Fill in the table with each food item and its sodium content. Add up your daily total at the bottom.)

	Food Item	Sodium Content (mg)
Breakfast		
Snack		
Lunch		
Snack		
Dinner		
Snack		
Medicines		
Total:		

Daily Sodium Tracker

(Fill in the table with each food item and its sodium content. Add up your daily total at the bottom.)

	Food Item	Sodium Content (mg)
Breakfast		
Snack		
Lunch		
Snack		
Dinner		
Snack		
Medicines		
Total:		

Symptom Tracker

(Fill in the table with your sodium intake for the day and write down any symptoms you have.)

Date	Sodium Intake	Symptoms

Symptom Tracker

(Fill in the table with your sodium intake for the day and write down any symptoms you have.)

Date	Sodium Intake	Symptoms

Symptom Tracker

(Fill in the table with your sodium intake for the day and write down any symptoms you have.)

Date	Sodium Intake	Symptoms

Symptom Tracker

(Fill in the table with your sodium intake for the day and write down any symptoms you have.)

Date	Sodium Intake	Symptoms

Symptom Tracker

(Fill in the table with your sodium intake for the day and write down any symptoms you have.)

Date	Sodium Intake	Symptoms

Symptom Tracker

(Fill in the table with your sodium intake for the day and
write down any symptoms you have.)

Date	Sodium Intake	Symptoms

ABOUT THE AUTHOR

Jennifer Brannon is a Pediatrician, wife, and mother of three. Her journey into eating a low-sodium diet started with her diagnosis of Menière's disease in 2015. Achieving a daily sodium intake of 1,500mg or less was challenging for her, despite her medical and nutritional knowledge. After much research and trial and error, the idea for this book was born. She hopes to help those trying to lower their sodium intake by providing some very practical, easy to understand ideas, as well as specific names of products and restaurants for those trying to reduce sodium in their diet.

To see more from this author, go to

https://www.facebook.com/JenniferBrannonAuthor/

Made in the USA
Lexington, KY
29 April 2019